THE HERB BASKET

Sage

Sorrel & Savory

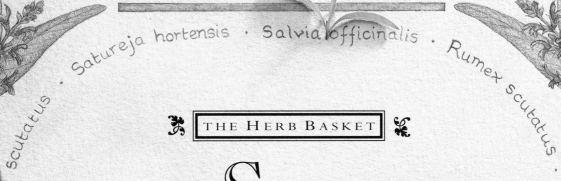

THE HERB BASKET

Sage

Sorrel & Savory

PHOTOGRAPHY BY GLORIA NICOL

Text by Hazel Evans

JG PRESS

Satureja hortensis · Salvia officinalis · Rumex scutatus · Salvia officinalis · Rumex scutatus · Satureja hortensis

THE HERB BASKET
Sage, Sorrel, and Savory

Designed and created by
THE BRIDGEWATER BOOK COMPANY LTD.

Written by Hazel Evans
Photography by Gloria Nicol

Designer: Jane Lanaway
Project editors: Veronica Sperling/Christine McFadden
Page makeup: Chris Lanaway
Step illustrations: Vana Haggerty
Border illustration: Pauline Allen
Cover: Annie Moss
American adaptation: Josephine Bacon

CLB 4497
© 1996 COLOUR LIBRARY BOOKS LTD
Published in the USA 1996 by JG Press
Distributed by World Publications, Inc.

The JG Press imprint is a trademark of
JG Press, Inc., 455 Somerset Avenue,
North Dighton, MA 02764
All rights reserved.

Color separation by Tien Wah Press
Printed and bound in Singapore by Tien Wah Press

ISBN 1-57215-113-7

CONTENTS

Rumex scutatus · Salvia officinalis · Satureja hortensis

THE JOY OF HERBS

Sage

Sorrel

Savory

RAGRANT, COLORFUL herbs are not only among the most enchanting plants in any garden but also the most useful. They appeal to all our senses, even that of touch, with their wide range of shapes and textures.

Herbs have come down to us through history, but over the years we have lost much of the valuable knowledge of how to prepare, preserve, and use them. Instead we have come to rely almost entirely on stores and markets for our food and drink, medicines, and beauty preparations. However, today, herbs are having a great revival, as people realise what a vital part they have to play in our lives. There is nothing difficult about growing and using these helpful plants. If you can grow garden flowers then aromatics follow easily. If you can follow a recipe then you'll have no problems about making a fragrant potpourri, putting it out in bowls to perfume a room. Added to your food or steeped in oils and vinegars, herbs bring sunshine indoors all winter long. And they offer so much more. They will scent your bath, soothe aching limbs, make calming teas to sip on a summer evening, and not only decorate your house but also keep insects at bay.

There is nothing more pleasant than to walk through your herb garden, however small it may be, at dusk on a summer's day, picking a leaf here and there, taking in the scents and perfumes, choosing what to use with a salad or a cooked dish. Even if you have no garden, you can still enjoy their company, for herbs will happily accommodate themselves on a windowsill, rewarding you not just with instant flavor for your food, but also scent and color. For herbs are not just our servants, they are also companionable plants – try for yourself and see. Discover exciting new ways that these unique plants can add flavor to your food, and fragrance to your home.

SAGE, SORREL, AND SAVORY

LEFT TO RIGHT

Savory, sage, and sorrel.

11

Salvia
officinalis
Tricolor

Salvia
officin...
Purpurea

Salvia
lavandulifolia

Salvia
rutilans

Sa...
off...
icterin...

Salvia
sclarea

Sage comes in many
attractive guises.

Salvia
officinalis

INTRODUCING SAGE

THE WORD SAGE comes from the Latin *salvere*, to be saved or preserved, while the English name refers to wisdom. The Romans considered sage to be sacred and it has always been rated as one of the great healing herbs of all time. There is an old belief that where sage flourishes in a garden the woman rules, and another that the plant grows or withers according to the prosperity of the master of the house.

Known to promote a long and healthy life, the 18th-century writer John Evelyn said it was a plant "endu'd with so many wonderful properties as that the assiduous use of it is said to render men immortal." The ancient Chinese thought so highly of it that they would trade three chests of China tea (the dried leaves of a form of *Camellia*) for one of sage leaves.

"How can man grow old who has sage in his garden?" says an ancient proverb. There is also a saying that "he that would live for aye, must eat Sage in May." Italian peasants to this day eat it in that month to preserve their health. It is also said to improve brain power.

Found growing in wild profusion in its native habitat, the Mediterranean, sage can stand on its own as a decorative plant in any flowerbed and will survive the winter.

CHINA TEA

Tea is made from an evergreen shrub called Camellia thea. *The leaves are picked, air-dried, then roasted, rolled, then dried again. The flowery taste of some China teas comes from the addition of dried jasmine flowers.*

13

SAGE, SORREL, AND SAVORY

There are more than 700 different kinds of sage, many of them purely decorative garden plants. The usual herb garden form, *Salvia officinalis*, has gray-green foliage and purple-blue flowers, but there are many others to choose from.

COMMON GARDEN SAGE
Salvia officinalis

This is the traditional sage grown in most English gardens. It is the variety most used for cooking, especially aromatic stuffings.

PURPLE SAGE
Salvia officinalis purpurescens

This is a shrubby form of sage with red-purple leaves. The leaves have a strong flavor and are used in herbal medicine. It is especially prized as a cure for sore throats. There is also a variegated version of purple sage, *purpurescens variegata*, which looks very attractive.

GOLD SAGE
Salvia officinalis "Icterina"

This sage has a milder flavor than the more widely used one, and is worth growing for dishes in which you need just a touch of the herb. Its leaves are bright green splashed with gold, which makes it a decorative choice for a herb garden.

SAGE IN A BORDER

Sage is such a decorative plant that it looks good in a border. The purple variety, Salvia officinalis purpurescens *is shown here, picking up the color of the chive flowers nearby. Try using tricolor sage,* Salvia officinalis "tricolor" *among bedding plants like geraniums and petunias.*

14

TRICOLOR SAGE
Salvia officinalis "tricolor"

This very decorative sage has cream-edged leaves splashed with pink. It does not grow very tall and is inclined to be tender, so may need shelter from hard frosts. Raised from cuttings, it makes a pretty candidate to grow in a pot.

NARROW-LEAVED SAGE
Salvia officinalis lavandulifolia

This narrow-leaved sage comes from Spain and has leaves that look like those of lavender. The Spaniards drink it as a health-giving tea. It can be grown from seed in late spring.

CLARY SAGE
Salvia sclarea

This sage looks completely different from the rest. It has broad, flat leaves and tall bristly stems which produce attractive white, lavender, and pink flower spikes from early summer to late fall. It is used widely in the French perfumery industry as a source of muscatel oil, despite the rather unpleasant smell that comes from its leaves. Unsuitable for use in the kitchen, it grows 3 feet or more in height.

RIGHT *Sage as part of a dried arrangement.*

A VERSATILE HERB

Sage has many home uses, from a gargle to a rinse for dark hair. Its aromatic leaves are excellent with poultry and some meats. But unless you have made a sage-and-onion stuffing for roast chicken with fresh sage leaves, you have missed something special. It is splendid, too, as a foil for greasy foods like duck and goose. It is one of the favorite herbs of the Italians who feature it in many of their classic dishes such as saltimbocca.

INTRODUCING SORREL

SORREL GETS its name from the old French word "*surelle*" which means sour. And that just about sums up the sharp taste of the plant. The plant used to be called "cuckoo's meate" (*pain de coucou* in French) because it was believed by country people that cuckoos feasted on it to clear their throats.

In the time of Henry VIII, sorrel was a favorite vegetable at the king's court. Some people believe, incidentally, that it was the tiny leaves of wood sorrel rather than the shamrock, which St Patrick, the patron saint of Ireland, used to demonstrate the trinity. John Evelyn wrote in 1720 that sorrel "cools the liver… and in the making of sallets imparts a greatful quickness to the rest as supplying the want of oranges and lemons."

Sorrel's distinctive lemony flavor has come back into favor in recent years for fashionable sauces in the *Nouvelle Cuisine* mode. Tasting something like spinach but with a much stronger citrus kick, it needs to be used in small quantities as a flavoring rather than as a vegetable. It is very difficult to find in the stores and markets but can be grown with great ease in your garden. Buckler leaf or French sorrel, *Rumex scutatus* has wider leaves like arrowheads, and is preferred by some for its milder flavor.

Sorrel comes from the dock family, which includes rhubarb. Use its sharp flavor as a refreshing counterfoil to rich creamy food, as the Romans did. It makes an attractive sauce to go with greasy foods like duck or goose. Laplanders use it instead of rennet to curdle milk for making cheese.

Try it as a cooling drink: Culpeper claimed that it refreshed "overspent spirits."

COOLING DRINK

Sorrel is seldom served as a drink these days because its rather sharp, acrid taste is harsh on the tongue – but try this refreshing beverage. Make up a solution of one tablespoonful of minced leaves in six tablespoons of boiling water. Allow it to steep, strain, then mix with a bottle of white wine.

Left to run to seed, sorrel's dark-green leaves make a handsome backdrop to lovage and chives.

SAGE, SORREL, AND SAVORY

INTRODUCING SAVORY

SHRUBBY SAVORY, with its distinctive peppery taste is a native of the Mediterranean where it grows wild on the hillsides. The Romans grew it near their beehives in the hope of getting some much prized savory honey which they used as an aphrodisiac. They used savory vinegar (see page 42) in the way we use mint sauce today with lamb, and their armies were responsible for bringing it to northern Europe.

There are two kinds of savory, the summer variety (*Satureia hortensis*) and the perennial winter variety (*Satureia montana*), and both of them come from the southern countries of Europe. Both kinds of savory were on the list of plants taken across the Atlantic to the United States by the Pilgrim Fathers. Winter savory is often grown in gardens today as a useful edging plant for a summer border. It can also be found as a creeping version (*Satureia montana reprandra*), which looks good on rockeries.

Culpeper wrote that it "Quickens dull spirits in lethargy" while Parkinson suggested mixing dry savory with breadcrumbs to give a "quicker relish to fish and meat". An adaption of his recipe is on page 39. The finer of the two varieties, and the one most used in cooking, is summer savory which has a distinctive peppery, rather bitter flavor, not unlike that of thyme. It is used traditionally with beans of any kind, and gives an extra zing to fresh pea soup. In Italy it is used in sausage-making, especially the famous salami. Above all, it is often used to partner goat's cheese with which it seems to have a particular affinity.

Widely used at one time in medicine for everything from poor eyesight to tinnitus, it is still grabbed by gardeners today as an emergency treatment for wasp- or bee-stings.

SAGE, SORREL, AND SAVORY

Pot-grown savories make handsome indoor

PLANT CARE

SAGE
Salvia officinalis

S AGE IS A perennial plant and an evergreen and will grow to a height of around 2 feet. It likes a fertile soil if it can get it, and some sun, but otherwise will survive in almost any garden surroundings, as long as the ground is well drained. And, provided you cut it back to base in the spring, it will turn in time into a small, good-looking bush that will flourish for many years.

Sow common and clary sage in the spring where they are to grow. Take cuttings from the variegated varieties as they do not always grow true to form from seed. Plant out the cuttings in the fall. Old sage plants which have become "leggy" can be layered very successfully by pegging a branch down and covering it with soil. Plants need to be replaced every 4–7 years.

1. Take cuttings from mid-summer to the end of summer. Using a clean sharp knife, cut off a non-flowering sideshoot 4–6 inches long. Cut off the stem just below a set of leaves.

2. Dip the end of the cutting in water then in rooting powder, shake off the excess, and plant the cutting firmly in a pot of suitable compost.

SORREL
Rumex acetosa, Rumex scutatus

ORREL, *R. acetosa,* is a lush green perennial which usually grows up to 18 inches high but can reach 2 feet in a wet summer. Sorrel will grow almost anywhere but prefers a moist acid soil and some shade.

Sow the seed in spring and thin the seedlings out to 9 inches apart as they grow. A little sorrel goes a long way – a dozen plants will be more than enough. As the flowers appear, cut the stems to the ground and fresh shoots will appear. Divide the plants regularly in spring or fall, as if they become too tightly packed, they will attract the attention of snails. French or buckler leaf sorrel, *R. scutatus,* grows to a height of 12–18 inches. Unlike *R. acetosa,* it prefers a dry soil. Sow the seed in shallow drills, then thin the seedlings first to 3 inches then to 6 inches apart as they grow. Pinch out the tiny green flowers to encourage new growth.

1. *To thin the seedlings, lift and replant 9 inches apart, taking care not to damage the delicate roots. Alternatively, simply uproot unwanted seedlings for use in salads.*

SAVORY
Satureia montana, Satureia hortensis

INTER SAVORY, *S. montana,* is a shrubby perennial that keeps its leaves on most of the year round. It grows to a height of about 12 inches tall and likes to be in full sun in a well-drained soil.

Sow the seed where it is to grow in early fall or in the spring. Thin the seedlings to 6–9 inches apart when they are large enough to handle. Alternatively, divide the roots in early spring, or take cuttings in early summer. Winter savory needs to be replaced every 2–3 years as it becomes very woody.

Summer savory, *S. hortensis,* is a half-hardy annual which grows from 8–12 inches high. Like winter savory, it prefers the sun and it must have a well-drained soil. Sow summer savory in the spring where it is to grow. For a winter supply, sow in the early fall to grow in pots in the greenhouse. Although summer savory is an annual, once you have raised a patch from seed it will self-sow from then onward, giving you a fresh crop of plants each spring.

TIP
Take cuttings of winter savory in the fall, pot them up, and bring them indoors for fresh young growth in winter.

21

HARVESTING

THE BEST TIME for collecting herbs is late morning on a sunny, warm day after the dew has dried. Never pick plants that are wet and always check them out for insects. Any plant that is going to be used for cooking must be one that has not been sprayed with herbicide or insecticide.
Don't stuff your herbs into a bag, you will crush them and release some of their valuable essential oils. Lay them out gently in a wide, flat basket.
Don't pick more than you can deal with at one time.
Pick leaves when the flowers on the plant are still in bud, don't strip too many off the stem or you may damage it. Pick flowers just before they open.

LEFT *The freshly-harvested leaves of sage can be added sparingly to tomato dishes and stews.*

HARVESTING SAGE

The best time to cut the fresh stems is in early summer – sage leaves can turn leathery later on. Plants that have flowered will have lost some of their pungent power. Inspect the leaves for any insects or signs of disease. Once sage has become twiggy, you can pick some sprigs and keep them on hand in the kitchen, helping yourself to leaves when you need them.

TIP
After you have cut down your sorrel plants, watch for the first fresh green tips and snip them off to use in salads.

HARVESTING SORREL

Pick only the fresh, young succulent leaves of sorrel as you want to use them, or freeze them right away. Sorrel is at its best in early summer, later on the leaves tend to become bitter. Inspect the leaves for baby snails which love to lurk on their undersides, and rinse them thoroughly before using. Tear off the stems, which can be stringy and tough, and use only the leaves in cookery. The leaves cook very quickly, turning to a purée almost immediately.

HARVESTING SAVORY

Harvest savory in the early morning before the heat of the midday sun leaches out the natural oils. Then hang bunches of sprigs in the shade for the dew to dry off them before packing them away. Pick savory leaves when they are relatively young. The older stems, which can become leathery towards the end of summer, are best used for decoration – on top of small cheeses for instance.

LEFT *Always deal with sorrel leaves the moment you harvest them.*

23

Bunches of drying herbs look attractive in the kitchen.

PRESERVING

ERBS CAN BE preserved in many ways. The more pungent varieties are good steeped in oil, while others, including sorrel, can be packed between layers of salt. Don't forget to use them, too, in pickles and chutneys. They should always be added toward the end of the cooking process.

PRESERVING SAGE

As sage is a perennial plant you can pick it all year round without having to resort to drying it, but some people prefer the stronger flavor that dried leaves give.

Strip away any leaves on the stems you have cut that may be turning yellow, and tie the sage in bundles of five or six stems at a time. Hang the bundles, tips down, in a dry, warm place such as near a furnace or radiator or on a shady porch in summer. After about a week the leaves should be dry and crisp. They can then be crumbled by hand, or sieved then stored in screw-top jars.

You may want to dry decorative variegated sage, purple sage, or tricolor sage for part of a winter flower arrangement. The easiest way to do this is to choose some long stems and simply put them in a jar with no water. Kept in a warm, well-ventilated place away from the light, they will dry out very successfully and will make an attractive display.

PRESERVING SORREL

Sorrel cannot be dried but can be frozen very successfully. Simply blanch the leaves briefly in boiling water, drain them, pat them partly dry between two pieces of kitchen paper towel, then pack them in plastic bags. As the flavor of sorrel is so pungent, it pays to mark the weight of the fresh-picked leaves on the packet to make sure you do not add too much to a dish and overwhelm it.

PRESERVING SAVORY

Savory does not dry particularly well, and is best frozen. The easiest way to do this is to strip the tiny leaves off the stems, fill ice cube trays with them, top up with water, and freeze. You then have cubes of flavor to use in broths, soups, and stews. Alternatively take whole sprigs and pack them in plastic sandwich bags and store them in the freezer.

SAGE, SORREL, AND SAVORY

AN HERBAL KNOT

Mint ——————

————— Thyme

Purple sage ——————

————— Tricolor sage

Chives ——————

————— Golden sage

————— Marjoram

SAGES IN ALL their variety, and savories, are both well-tempered plants to use in a herbal knot. This design, which is based on an Elizabethan pattern, uses mainly low growers.

Herbs take perfectly to pots which are often the solution if you want essential items like mint, chives, and sage growing to hand near the kitchen door. There's a wide choice of new and re-cycled containers around that they would grow happily in, ranging from an old gasoline can painted Mediterranean blue, to the most expensive stone urn.

The traditional terracotta pot looks particularly good against the green-and-yellow foliage of herbs but is inclined to be fragile and because it is porous, needs watering more often. Plastic is the cheapest and the most popular. It is lightweight, does not break easily, and keeps the soil moist. Glass fiber can be molded and colored to imitate lead and stone. It is light, keeps the compost moist, and is strong and long-lasting. Reconstituted stone makes good imitations of traditional urns and vases but is heavy to move around.

Keep sage plants clipped to get a good, bushy appearance.

SAGE, SORREL, AND SAVORY

AN HERBAL TOWER

◉ NE OF THE most attractive ways of getting a number of herbs into a relatively small space is to grow an herbal tower. A strawberry-barrel can just as easily be an herb-barrel, or you could use clay strawberry-pots on a smaller scale. Or you could make your own tower using a large plastic garbage bag. If the plastic is relatively thin, use two, one inside the other.

HIGH-RISE HERBS

There are many kinds of flower towers on the market now that do equally well for herbs. Some slot into one another to make mini-skyscrapers, others can be fixed to a wall, or allowed to hang from a bracket. Try making your own, use your ingenuity - a discarded linen basket could have holes cut in its sides to take plants, a piece of plastic drainpipe could easily have holes bored in it too, for the same purpose.

LEFT *Try growing herbs in a strawberry pot.*

1. *Decide where the tower is to go, site the bag, and fill with good quality compost, rolling down the top of the bag to the required height. Make drainage holes in the bottom and sit it on pieces of tile so there is a gap between the bag and the ground. If you are using a large bag, put a piece of drainpipe down the center temporarily, and fill it with pebbles or stones. As you fill the compost around it, pull the pipe up, and eventually out. This gives the bag a very effective drainage system.*

2. *Using sharp scissors, make holes in the side where you want the herbs to go, creating a diamond pattern. Then push in the herbs, roots first. In time they should cover the plastic.*

TIP

When planting any kind of herb-barrel or tower, it is vital that you make sure that it is placed on level ground. Otherwise you will find when you water it that one side will get plenty of moisture while the other may go without.

SAGE, SORREL, AND SAVORY

HERBAL EDGES

BOTH SORREL and winter savory make good tight-packed miniature edging for an herb plot. Clip the savory regularly so that it bushes out and knits into a tidy, miniature hedge. The sorrel will make a lush green fringe round a patch of herbs but would look equally good around a herbaceous border. Put your plants closer together than you would normally – half the distance apart. Water them well when you put them in. Once they are established, divide and re-plant them from time to time.

ABOVE *Sorrel's broad leaves make an attractive edging plant.*

PLANTING AND WATERING

WHAT ALL herbs need is good drainage. Make sure that any containers you use have a thick layer of stones or pebbles in the bottom to allow excess moisture to drain below soil level when you water them. Basil, in particular, hates to have wet feet. Watering your herbs from the top should only be done when the sun goes down, and when there is no frost expected. Change the soil every year – your herbs will have leached all the nutrients out in the space of one summer. And use a soil-based bedding mixture as lighter ones will tend to make growing plants top-heavy and they will be blown over in the wind. Group your herbs together – they're happiest that way.

SAGE, SORREL, AND SAVORY

Unrestrained savory makes an attractive flowering edge to a plot.

SALADS

S AGE, SORREL, and savory all make lively additions to a salad. As they all have pungent flavors, however, they should be used sparingly or they may overwhelm the other ingredients. For best results, always choose good quality olive oil to dress salads.

32

SORREL AND POTATO SALAD

INGREDIENTS

Serves 4

1 Boston lettuce

8 ounces waxy potatoes

4 tbs olive oil

1 small onion

4 tbs shredded sorrel

1 tbs white wine vinegar

½ tsp French mustard

❖ Wash and dry the lettuce. Tear it into pieces and put in a salad bowl.
❖ Wash the potatoes and cook them in their skins. When cool enough to handle, peel and slice thickly, and put them in a separate bowl. Pour 1 tablespoon of the olive oil over the potatoes while they are still warm, and toss. Chop the onion and stir in.
❖ When the potatoes are cool, pile them on top of the lettuce and scatter with shreds of sorrel.
❖ Beat the remaining olive oil into the vinegar, stir in the mustard, season, and pour over the salad just before serving.

COUNTRY SALAD

INGREDIENTS

Serves 4

8 cups fresh spinach

2 tbs shredded sorrel

1 onion

4 slices ham

handful of cherry tomatoes

¼ cup walnut halves

1 tbs chopped sage

1 tbs chopped savory

Parmesan cheese

8 tbs vinaigrette

1 tsp French mustard

❖ Wash the spinach well, pat dry, and tear into pieces, mixing in the sorrel leaves.
❖ Slice the onion into rings and separate them.
❖ Cut the ham into slivers. Scatter the onion rings and ham over the salad.
❖ Add the cherry tomatoes, walnuts, sage, and savory.
❖ Grate a generous helping of Parmesan cheese over the salad.
❖ Mix the vinaigrette with the mustard, pour over, and toss well.

TIP

It is often difficult to keep summer salads looking good in hot weather, especially if the ingredients are store bought rather than from the garden. If you find your salad leaves are tending to flag, put them in a bowl with a handful of ice-cubes to revive them. Always add the dressing at the last possible moment.

ROAST PORK WITH SAGE

PORK AND SAGE make a perfect partnership, particularly if a sharp flavor of citrus, wine, or cider is added. Try coating pork fillets in egg then dipping them into a mix of breadcrumbs with a little dried sage and grated lemon rind. The result is delicious!

PORK WITH SAGE BUTTER SAUCE

SAGE BUTTER is used here to thicken a piquant, cider vinegar-based sauce. Cook it very gently, otherwise the sauce will separate. Allow plenty of time for marinating the pork in the cider-and-herb mixture – at least four hours, but overnight would be better.

INGREDIENTS

Serves 4

2 tbs sage leaves
1 small onion
3 tbs olive oil
6 tbs cider vinegar
1 bayleaf
sprig of thyme
2½ pounds pork loin
2 tbs Sage Butter (page 38)
1 tbs sage flowers
sugar (optional)

❖ Finely chop the sage leaves and peel and mince the onion. Combine with the olive oil and 4 tablespoons of the cider vinegar. Add the bayleaf, thyme, and pork, then marinate in the refrigerator for as long as possible, turning occasionally.

❖ Wrap the pork and the marinade tightly in a large piece of aluminum foil or a roasting-bag, removing the thyme and the bay.

❖ Place in a roasting pan and cook in a preheated oven at 325 degrees for 1½ hours.

❖ Unwrap the pork, and drain the juices into a small saucepan. Add the remaining vinegar and the sage butter to the pan and cook gently for about 10 minutes, until the butter has melted and the sauce has thickened a little. Taste the sauce and add a little sugar if ncessary.

❖ Slice the pork, pour the sauce over it and garnish with sage flowers.

REAL SAGE-AND-ONION STUFFING

SAGE IS THE basic ingredient in most packet stuffings, but try making your own with fresh leaves and you'll be delighted with the difference. Savory can be used in a stuffing or dressing too, for a different flavor.

INGREDIENTS

Serves 4
1 onion
butter
fresh breadcrumbs
3 tbs minced fresh sage or 2 tsp dried sage
1 large egg
4 tbs milk

❖ Peel and mince the onion.
❖ Melt the butter in a skillet and gently fry the onion for about 7 minutes or until slightly colored.
❖ Remove the pan from the heat and stir in the breadcrumbs. Add salt and pepper to taste, and stir in the minced sage.
❖ Beat the egg lightly.
❖ Add the milk and stir into the mix.
❖ Use to stuff a pork roast, or cook and serve as an accompaniment.

TIP
Always save leftover scraps of bread. Grind them in a food processor to reduce them to crumbs then freeze them in plastic bags to use in stuffings.

Rumex scutatus · Salvia officinalis · Satureja hortensis ·
Rumex scutatus · Salvia officinalis · Satureja hortensis ·
Satureja hortensis · Rumex scutatus · Satureja hortensis ·
Salvia officinalis · Rumex scutatus · Satureja hortensis ·

SAGE, SORREL, AND SAVORY

RICH SAVORY STUFFING

T RY THIS savory stuffing as an alternative to one made with sage. It comes from an old country recipe. Use as an appetizing stuffing for pork loin or to serve with cold poultry. It goes well with trout too.

INGREDIENTS

Serves 4

4 slices bacon

¼ cup butter

1 onion, minced

2 cups finely chopped mushrooms

1 tbs minced savory

1 cup fresh breadcrumbs

1 egg

❖ Cut off the rind and finely chop the bacon.

❖ Melt half the butter in a skillet, add the bacon and onion, and cook slowly until the bacon fat runs out and the ingredients start to brown.

❖ Increase the heat, add the remaining butter and the mushrooms, and cook until any excess moisture has gone.

❖ Turn the mix into a large bowl, and stir in the savory and breadcrumbs. Beat the egg and add enough to bind into a firm mix. Season well.

T I P
For a variation on conventional stuffing, try substituting an equal quantity of boiled, well-drained rice for the breadcrumbs.

HERB BUTTERS

ERB BUTTERS are very easy to make and will store for a long time in the refrigerator, indefinitely in the freezer. Make a selection to keep on hand. Chill the butter, cut and wrap in small segments, or save in small pots so that you can defrost it quickly and easily to liven up a meal. A pot of chilled herb butter is delicious on broiled steak or chicken, and on fish too. The flavor is released as the butter melts and mingles with the cooking juices.

SAVORY BUTTER

Spread this butter on bread to go with cheeses of all kinds. Savory goes well with garlic, so add some to the mix if the idea appeals to you.

INGREDIENTS

Makes ¹/₂ cup
¹/₂ cup butter
2 tbs minced savory

❖ Melt the butter slowly in a saucepan, add the chopped savory, and cook for two minutes, stirring constantly. Take the pan off the heat, and leave to stand for 30 minutes.
❖ Reheat and strain off the herb. Pour the butter into little ceramic pots and decorate with fresh sprigs of savory.

SAGE BUTTER

It is best to used dried rather than fresh sage for this butter, otherwise the texture of fresh leaves makes it difficult to spread.

INGREDIENTS

Makes ¹/₂ cup
¹/₂ cup butter
1 tsp lemon juice
2 tsp dried sage

❖ Soften the butter with a fork and work in the lemon juice drop by drop, then the dried sage. Put the mix in the refrigerator to chill until firm.
❖ Turn out onto parchment or wax paper, and shape into a square before serving. Or cut into strips, wrap each one separately, and freeze.

SAGE, SORREL, AND SAVORY

SAGE, SORREL, AND SAVORY

SAGE LIQUEUR

SAGE HAS BEEN used traditionally by country people throughout the centuries to make refreshing drinks. Sage liqueur is often made in Provence where it is taken either as an *aperitif* to stimulate the appetite or as a *digestif* to settle the stomach.

INGREDIENTS

Makes 2 quarts
handful of sage leaves and flowers
2¼ pints vodka
2 cups sugar
2 cups water

❖ Fill a wide-mouthed jar with sage leaves and flowers, add the vodka, then cover and leave for 1 week.
❖ Slowly dissolve the sugar in the water over a low heat, then boil until it thickens to a syrup.
❖ Remove from the heat and leave to cool.
❖ Stir into the vodka/sage mix and leave for a further 5 days.
❖ Strain into clean bottles.

TIP
Herb liqueurs always need careful straining if they are to have a jewel-like clarity of color. Leave the bottle upright for the debris to drop to the bottom, then pour off the liquid through cheesecloth, leaving the lees behind.

40

ROSÉ SAGE APERITIF

CHAUCER WROTE that you should drink sage wine for "dark ulterior motives." The French, however, take it purely for pleasure as an *apéritif*. This is another traditional Provençal drink, using the delicious local rosé wine. Use purple sage for it if you can, as it will give the finished wine an even deeper pink tinge.

INGREDIENTS

Makes 1 quart
1 bottle rosé wine
½ cup white wine
3 small sprigs fresh sage
2 tbs clear honey

❖ Put the wines and the sage into a jar with a tight-fitting lid and leave in a cool dark place to steep for a fortnight.
❖ Strain the wine into a bowl and stir in the honey.
❖ Transfer the mixture to a clean bottle and seal tightly. Store in a cool place.

TIP
If you substitute purple sage, *Salvia officinalis purpurescens*, for the conventional green-leaved variety when making this aperitif, the drink will take on an attractive rich dark coloring similar to port.

OILS AND VINEGARS

ERB OILS and vinegars have many uses, not all of them culinary. Use sage vinegar not just in food but as a beauty product as well - brush some through your hair regularly or use it as a rinse to make your hair shine and to cover grey hairs. Sage oil can be used beneficially in a relaxing massage for aching limbs.

HERB VINEGAR

HIS OLD recipe for herb vinegar can be made at any time of year as it does not need the warmth of the sun to bring out the aromatic qualities of the herbs. If you do not want to follow the phases of the moon, simply leave your herb vinegar for six weeks before using.

❧ Begin on the day of the new moon. Fill a wide-mouthed glass jar full of fresh sage or savory, or a mix of the two. Cover the herbs with top-quality cider vinegar that has just been warmed, not heated, to boiling point. Fill the jar to the brim, stir, and push in a cork or screw on a lid.
❧ Keep your herb vinegar in a dark cool place, and leave it there until the second new moon.
❧ Then strain the vinegar into a fresh jar and add a sprig of herb for decoration.

HERB OIL

ERB OILS are very easy to make, and in decorative bottles make good presents. Make them in summer when you can use the warmth of the sun to infuse the plants' essential oils. Store goats' cheeses in savory oil to give them extra flavor.

❧ Fill a sterilized jar full of sage or sorrel leaves. Pour olive oil over them and stir well with a knife to make sure no air pockets are left.
❧ Place an airtight cover on the jar and allow the mixture to steep in the sun.
❧ After two weeks, strain off the leaves, and start again with a fresh supply.
❧ After one month, the oil can be strained into another jar, and used to add flavor to salads and sauces.

SAGE, SORREL, AND SAVORY

To make sage vinegar you need a wide-mouthed glass jar with a screw top and some cider vinegar. Fill the jar with sage leaves, warm the vinegar in a saucepan, and pour it over them. Leave it for three weeks before straining the vinegar off the leaves. Then rebottle, adding a fresh sprig for decoration.

TIP
Give your herb vinegars an extra kick by adding a small handful of spices. Mustard seed and dill seed, for instance, go with most flavors, as do dried chili peppers.

43

SAGE, SORREL, AND SAVORY

SAGE RELISH

THIS BOTTLED sauce used to be made in English convents in the 18th century. It was left out on a table, and each nun was encouraged to give the bottle a shake as she passed to help mix the liquid. Get your family to do the same.

INGREDIENTS

Makes 1½ cups

1 shallot, minced

1 tbs sage leaves or 1 tsp dried sage

2 tsp grated lemon rind

2 tsp salt

pinch of cayenne

pinch of ground ginger

1 tsp lemon juice

1½ cups red wine

❖ Mix all the ingredients and put them into a screw-topped bottle. Shake the bottle every day for two weeks so that it mixes thoroughly.

❖ Leave to stand so the sediment goes to the bottom, then carefully decant into a fresh bottle leaving the sediment behind. Keep refrigerated. Use in marinades for pork or chicken, and to flavor gravies and thick sauces.

HERB-FLAVORED MUSTARD

INGREDIENTS

Makes 1 cup

1 cup French, German or American mustard

1 tbs dry white wine

2 tbs finely chopped savory or sage

❖ Mix all the ingredients together and store in an airtight jar for as long as possible before using. This mustard can be served with its herbs or sieved and put into a fresh jar.

HOT HERB MUSTARD

INGREDIENTS

Makes ¾ cup

1½ cups mustard powder

cider or herb vinegar

1 tbs chopped sage or savory

❖ Make up ¾ cup hot mustard to a thick cream using cider or herb vinegar. Stir in the finely chopped sage or savory.

❖ Leave this to steep for a week, then strain and bottle.

TIP

If you want a milder flavor, you can stir in a little fresh heavy cream before serving.

SAVORY JELLY

T HIS SAVORY jelly uses apple juice as a quick and easy way to make a herb jelly. It avoids having to strain the mixture overnight. It goes well with turkey, game, ham, and other cold meats.

INGREDIENTS

Makes 1 quart

2 tbs chopped savory or 1 tbs dried savory
1 quart apple juice
1½ cups sugar
juice of 1 lemon
¾ cup liquid pectin

❖ Put the savory into a saucepan with the apple juice, sugar, and lemon juice.
❖ Bring to the boil. Stir until the sugar has dissolved, then stir in the pectin. Boil for 2 minutes, stirring all the time.
❖ Remove the pan from the heat and skim off any foam.
❖ Place a savory sprig in each sterilized jar, pour the jelly over it, and seal.

46

SAGE FLOWER JELLY

CAPTURE the flavor of sage flowers in this delicate and delicious jelly. Serve it with cold pork or ham as a change from redcurrant jelly. If sage flowers are not in season, substitute young leaves instead. Potted in a decorative jar, the jelly makes an attractive gift.

INGREDIENTS

Makes 4 cups

8 cups roughly chopped, unpeeled tart apples

4 cups water

1 cup sage flowers or minced leaves

sugar

TIP

Use this basic recipe to make other herb flower jellies, marjoram and thyme, for instance. Try a chive-flower jelly with lamb.

1. Put the apples in a saucepan with the water. Add the sage flowers and simmer until the apples are soft and pulpy. Put the mix into a jellybag and suspend over a bowl overnight until all the juice has run free.

2. Measure the juice, and put into a large saucepan with 1½ cups sugar to every 2½ cups juice. Stir until the sugar has dissolved, then bring to the boil and cook over a high heat until the jelly has reached setting point.

3. Pour the jelly over flowering sprigs of sage in sterilized jars. Store away from the light.

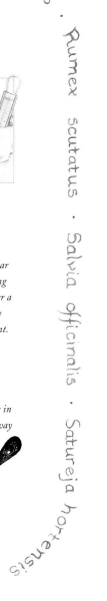

BARBECUE HERBS

I N MANY of the countries of the Middle East, sage is used in the classic kebob, with lamb, tomatoes, and onions. Thread young sage leaves onto skewers, alternating them with the other ingredients to give a delicious aroma while they cook, and a wonderful flavor when you eat them.

LAMB AND ZUCCHINI KEBOBS

INGREDIENTS

Serves 6

1½ pounds boned shoulder of lamb
1 shallot, finely chopped
1 clove garlic, crushed
2 tbs minced parsley
6 tbs olive oil
4 tbs sage vinegar or
dry white wine
2 tbs lemon juice
6 small zucchini
4 tbs butter
2 bayleaves
12 small salad tomatoes
6 small onions
3 tbs brandy
handful of
sage leaves

❖ Cut the lamb into 1-inch cubes. Mix the shallot with the garlic, parsley, olive oil, vinegar, lemon juice, and bayleaves. Add the meat and leave to marinate for half a day, then take out and leave to drain.

❖ Cut the zucchini into thick slices. Sauté them in the butter in a heavy-based skillet until they are just beginning to soften. Remove and drain.

❖ Grease 6 large skewers. Thread on the lamb, zucchini, and tomatoes, interlacing them with the sage leaves. Season with salt and pepper and brush with the butter remaining in the pan.

❖ Cook the kebobs 4 inches from the coals, turning from time to time, for up to 15 minutes or until the lamb is just cooked through.

❖ Arrange the kebobs on a flameproof dish, add the brandy, and ignite it.

❖ Serve with pita bread or plain white rice, accompanied by a tomato-and-onion salad.

BARBECUED PORK WITH SAVORY, SORREL, AND SAGE SAUCE

INGREDIENTS

Serves 8

6 tbs meat broth
1 tbs French mustard
6 tbs plain yogurt
juice of ½ lemon
1 tbs minced sage
2 tbs minced sorrel
1 tbs minced savory
⅔ cup mayonnaise
8 pork chops
salad of mixed green leaves, to serve

❖ Put the meat broth into a blender with the mustard, yogurt, lemon juice, sage, sorrel, and savory. Blend to a purée. Beat in the mayonnaise, and put into the refrigerator to chill.

❖ Broil the chops over hot coals for 10–12 minutes each side, until thoroughly cooked through.

❖ Serve them with the salad over which the sauce has been spooned.

TIP
If you are afraid that your barbecued meat may not cook right through, give it a few moments in a microwave oven immediately beforehand.

SAGE, SORREL, AND SAVORY

AN INDOOR TREE

THIS ATTRACTIVE topiary tree is made from oasis, a type of florist's foam which is easy to use. Dried sage twigs look very decorative in mixed dried flower arrangements, save some of the more decorative varieties to act as a foil for flowers and grasses.

MATERIALS

1 oasis ball about 5 inches
in diameter
1 cone-shaped piece of
oasis 7–8 inches tall
glue
thick bamboo or stout
straight twig at least
18 inches long
clay pot
polythene
plaster of Paris
spaghnum moss
dried sage twigs

1. *Slice a section from the ball and the base of the cone to create 2 flat surfaces of equal diameter, then glue them together.*

2. *Push the bamboo into the bottom of the ball. Line the pot with polythene. Make up a plaster of Paris mix and pour into the pot. Push the bamboo into the plaster and leave until set, making sure it is vertical.*

3. *Cover the oasis with spaghnum moss, glueing it in place, then glue the sage twigs in place to completely cover the tree. Trim the polythene and cover with moss.*

TIP
Save sage for potpourri too. The leaves help to bulk out a mixture, and their aroma mixes in well with more exotic scents.

SAGE, SORREL, AND SAVORY

SAGE FOR HEALTHY HAIR

N INFUSION of sage makes a rinse for brunettes that will help disguise grey hairs. Add some rosemary leaves to turn it into a hair tonic.

SAGE HAIR COLORANT

HIS MIX of sage and China tea helps to restore the colour of hair that is "pepper-and-salt" ie going gray. The color should last for six shampoos. It is advisable to do a test patch first, to make sure you like the color.

INGREDIENTS
China tea
1 tbs dried sage or 1tbs fresh sage

❖ Make up a strong brew of China tea.
❖ Add a tablespoonful of fresh sage or a teaspoonful of dried sage to the tea while it is still very hot.

❖ Allow to cool, strain, then, using rubber gloves so your hands are not stained, rub it into damp, shampooed hair with your fingertips.

SAGE AND ROSEMARY HAIR RINSE

N INFUSION of sage makes a rinse for brunettes that will help disguise gray hairs. Add some rosemary leaves to turn it into a hair tonic.

Make up a strong infusion of whole sage stems with their leaves on. Pour boiling water over them and bruise them with a wooden spoon. Strain and bottle when the mixture has cooled and refrigerate it. Rub a little into the roots of your hair each day.

SAGE, SORREL, AND SAVORY

A SAGE TOOTHPASTE FOR SMOKERS

This homemade toothpaste helps to remove nicotine stains from your teeth.

INGREDIENTS

fresh sage leaves
½ cup sea salt

❖ Take a handful of fresh sage leaves and crush them with ½ cup sea salt.
❖ Put the mix on a small baking sheet in a medium oven, until it bakes hard.
❖ Re-crush it and use the powder to clean your teeth.

SAGE VINEGAR RINSE

This rinse gives your hair highlights and an increased shine.

INGREDIENTS

Makes 5 ²⁄₃ cups
*²⁄₃ cup Sage Vinegar
(page 42)
5 cups water*

❖ Mix the vinegar and the water and pour it over your hair as a final rinse after shampooing. Use at least once a week.

53

HERBAL PLACE MATS

A POTPOURRI of dried herbs gives out a delicious aroma under a hot pan, plate, or teapot, if you encase the herbs in decorative mats. The mats are made from mattress ticking but you could use any other fabric you choose.

POTPOURRI

Makes 1

dried rind of 1 lemon

$1\frac{1}{2}$ cups dried rosemary

$1\frac{1}{2}$ cups dried thyme

2 cups dried sage

$1\frac{1}{2}$ cups dried savory

2 cinnamon sticks

1 tsp cloves

2 tbs orris root powder

$\frac{2}{3}$ cup dried pine needles

PLACE MATS

26 inches of mattress ticking 54 inches wide

piece of thin wadding 13 inches ×

9 inches

ruler

piece of dressmaking chalk

1. Mix together all the potpourri ingredients in a large bowl. Cut two pieces of ticking 13 inches by 9 inches, then trim to an oval shape. With wrong sides together, sandwich the wadding between them. Machine together $\frac{1}{4}$ in from the edge, leaving a quarter of one edge open. Stuff with a thick layer of potpourri, spreading it out evenly. Seam up the gap.

2. Using the ruler and chalk, mark out parallel diagonal lines to make a diamond pattern. Quilt through all three thicknesses of fabric, taking care not to dislodge the potpourri.

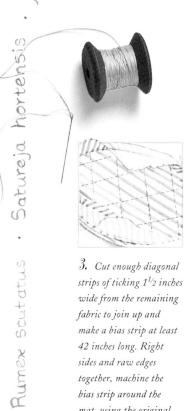

3. *Cut enough diagonal strips of ticking 1½ inches wide from the remaining fabric to join up and make a bias strip at least 42 inches long. Right sides and raw edges together, machine the bias strip around the mat, using the original stitching line as your guide. Fold over, press, then turn under and hem the remaining raw edge on the underside of the mat.*

TIP

You can also make an oval version of this mat, using pieces of ticking measuring 15 inches × 11 inches and drawing the oval shape freehand within the rectangle.

SAGE, SORREL, AND SAVORY

HERBAL DYES

ERBS HAVE been used for dyes and colorings ever since the days when the Ancient Britons painted themselves with woad. Sorrel has been used since medieval times to dye cloth. If you use the roots of sorrel you should get a dusky pink coloring, while the leaves and stems produce a subtle yellow. Use only natural fibers such as silk, wool, cotton, or linen for dying; man-made fibers simply will not "take."

⊹ First wash your material thoroughly. If you are using virgin wool you will need to wash it several times to remove the natural lanolin. End with a final rinse in vinegar.

⊹ You will need to add something to "fix" the color. Alum is the mordant that is normally used with sorrel. Buy it from a pharmacy, you will need 2 tbs for every 1 pound material.

⊹ Use an equal weight of sorrel to the weight of the fabric ie 1 pound herb to every 1 pound cloth.

⊹ Dissolve the alum in a little hot water, put it in a dye bath or bucket then add another 20 quarts water. Put in the fabric to be dyed, bring very slowly to the boil and simmer for one hour - the water temperature should be about 125 degrees. Rinse the fabric and it is ready for dyeing.

⊹ Chop the leaves of the sorrel or crush the roots with a hammer. Put it in a bag made from cheesecloth or a piece of old nylon net curtain.

Leave to soak overnight in a large preserving pan, enamel bowl, or bucket.

⊹ Then bring the mix to the boil and simmer for up to 3 hours, or until the water has taken on the color you want.

⊹ Take out the bag of sorrel, cool the mix then immerse the fabric and simmer for one hour.

⊹ Leave the fabric to cool in the water, then take out, and rinse in warm then cold water. Finally, hang out to dry.

TIP
If you are dyeing wool to make a sweater, always do an extra hank so you have yarn left for repairs. You will never be able to duplicate the exact shade again.

SAGE, SORREL, AND SAVORY

PRESSED HERB SACHETS

S AVORY IS just one of the many herbs that can be pressed to make attractive sachets. Try doing the same thing with small-leaved thymes, rosemary, or lavender. If you don't have a press, you can get equally good results using heavy books but mind how you close the pages, you don't want to disturb the sprigs. Use pressed herb sprigs, too, to decorate greetings cards. They also make good book-marks.

❖ Sprigs of savory press very well and make an attractive decoration for a herb sachet.
❖ Pick the savory just before you intend to press it. Make sure the leaves are clean and undamaged. Thin the sprays if necessary, using tweezers to remove individual leaves.
❖ Lay your leaves on absorbent paper such as plain kitchen paper towels, toilet tissue, paper tissues, or diaper liners, on top of several sheets of coarse paper. Cover with another piece of paper, making sure the leaves are not dislodged as you do so.
❖ Carefully place in a flower-press or between the pages of a heavy book, topping with more paper as you do so. Leave for about two weeks then inspect the savory to see how it is doing. The leaves should feel crisp. If it needs more time, replace the top papers.

TIP
The easiest way to handle the rather fragile, freshly-dried sprigs of herbs is to use a pair of tweezers. You can then pick them up and guide them into place without damaging them at all.

1. Make up a herb sachet by cutting two 5-inch squares of fabric. Right sides together, sew them round three sides, allowing ½ inch seam allowance. Fill them with potpourri, then turn in, and hand hem the remaining side. Finish off with a frill of narrow lace.

SAGE, SORREL, AND SAVORY

2. Mount the dried savory sprig on to the sachets using drops of a rubber-based glue, applied with a cocktail stick. Press in place with the palm of your hand. Leave the glue to dry, then spray the savory with extra-strong hair lacquer, held at a distance.
You can, if you like, add an extra layer of fine cheesecloth to the sachet before putting on the lace, letting it cover the savory sprig which will show through.

INDEX

ACKNOWLEDGMENTS

The publishers would like to thank
the following companies for their help:

BASKETS AND GLASSWARE
Global Village,
Sparrow Works, Bower Hinton, Martock, Somerset, UK
Telephone: +44(1935) 823390

DRIED HERBS AND FLOWERS
The Hop Shop,
Castle Farm, Shoreham, Sevenoaks, Kent TN14 7UB UK
Telephone: +44(1959) 523219

HERB PLANTS BY MAIL ORDER
Jekka's Herb Farm,
Rose Cottage, Shellards Lane, Alveston, Bristol BS12 2SY, UK
Telephone: +44(1454) 418878

HERB SEEDS
Suffolk Seeds,
Monks Farm, Pantlings Lane, Coggeshall Road,
Kelvedon, Essex CO5 9PG, UK
Telephone: +44(1376) 572456

PICTURE CREDITS
Harry Smith Horticultural Photographic Collection
p27, 28, 30, 31,

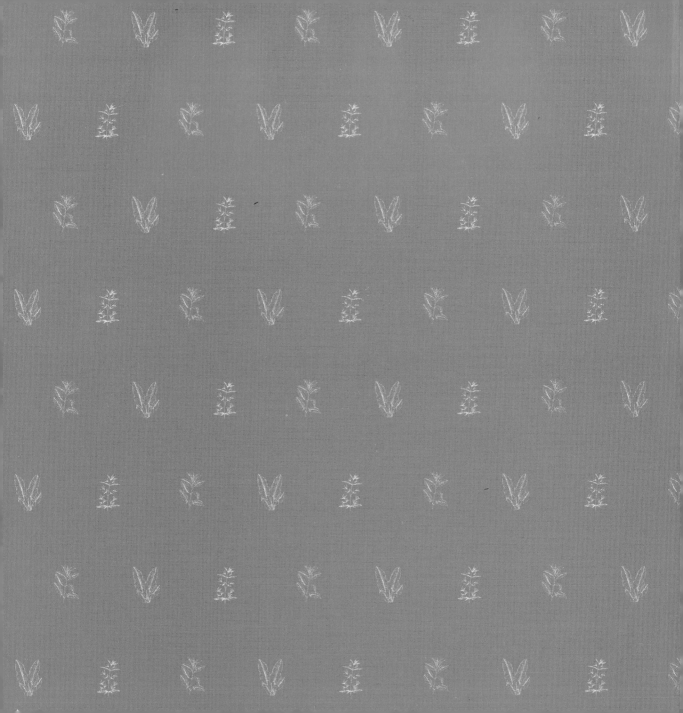